Francis George Heath

The fern portfolio. All the species of British ferns are included in

this volume

Francis George Heath

The fern portfolio. All the species of British ferns are included in this volume

ISBN/EAN: 9783742891631

Manufactured in Europe, USA, Canada, Australia, Japa

Cover: Foto ©Thomas Meinert / pixelio.de

Manufactured and distributed by brebook publishing software
(www.brebook.com)

Francis George Heath

The fern portfolio. All the species of British ferns are included in this volume

Heath's Fern Portfolio

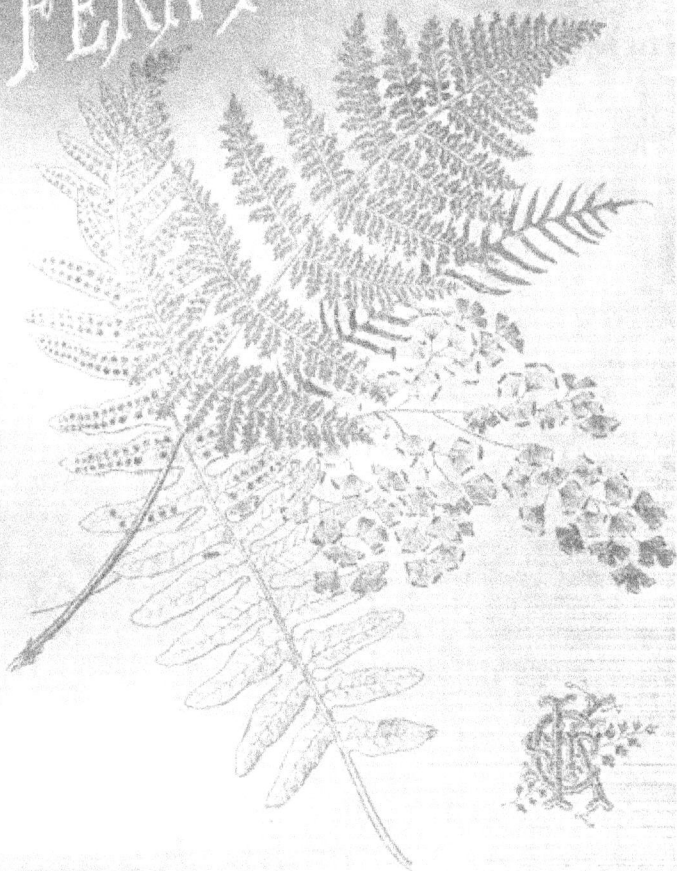

THE
FERN PORTFOLIO.

BY

FRANCIS GEORGE HEATH.

EDITOR OF
THE NEW EDITION OF GILPIN'S "FOREST SCENERY,"

AUTHOR OF

" *The Fern World*," " *The Fern Paradise*," " *Our Woodland Trees*," " *Autumnal Leaves*,"
" *Sylvan Spring*," " *Burnham Beeches*," " *Where to Find Ferns*,"
" *Trees and Ferns*," " *My Garden Wild*," " *Tree Gossip*,"
" *The English Peasantry*," " *Peasant Life*,"
Etc., Etc.

ALL THE SPECIES OF BRITISH FERNS ARE INCLUDED IN THIS VOLUME.

*PUBLISHED UNDER THE DIRECTION OF THE COMMITTEE OF GENERAL LITERATURE AND
EDUCATION, APPOINTED BY THE SOCIETY FOR PROMOTING
CHRISTIAN KNOWLEDGE.*

LONDON:
SOCIETY FOR PROMOTING CHRISTIAN KNOWLEDGE,
NORTHUMBERLAND AVENUE, CHARING CROSS, W.C.;
43, QUEEN VICTORIA STREET, E.C.; 26, ST. GEORGE'S PLACE, HYDE PARK CORNER, S.W.
BRIGHTON : 135, NORTH STREET.   NEW YORK : E. & J. B. YOUNG & CO.

1885.

INTRODUCTION.

THE aim of "THE FERN PORTFOLIO" is the production of a series of life-size representations of the fronds of Ferns, with accompanying letterpress descriptions. The text is intended to be quite subordinate to the plates. These it is the especial object of the work to render absolutely life-like pictures of the plants from which they are drawn; and infinite pains have been taken to attain this object.

A common, and it may, indeed, be said to be the general, method of botanical illustration is to give an approximate drawing of the outline of the leaf or frond of a plant, with a few "artistic" scratches, lightly dashed off, to indicate the course of the rnid and side, or branch, veins, and to throw colour in—where it is employed—with just shading enough to give an approximate idea of the hue; and *no attempt* has ever been made to produce an absolute *fac-simile*—in form, colour, and venation (by which is meant the veining, or system of veins) of a plant leaf or frond.

The Author of this volume was the first to attempt to depart from this common, and inexact, method of plant illustration; and in "OUR WOODLAND TREES," first published in 1878, he gave, in a series of eight plates, *fac-similes*, in outline, in veining, and in colour, of the leaves of British trees. In 1881 he published, in "AUTUMNAL LEAVES," another set of twelve plates, giving, on precisely the same plan, *fac-similes*, in the form of 252 figures, of autumn-tinted foliage. The high praise lavished by the entire British press upon these attempts to picture the exceeding beauty of the leaves of trees when in the height of their summer sheen, and when under the glow of their departing hues, furnished the inducement to represent Ferns in a similar manner, but with the difference that the fronds of the flowerless plants should be life-size. The leaf *fac-similes* in "OUR WOODLAND TREES" and in "AUTUMNAL LEAVES" were reduced in the drawings—to accommodate the latter to the size of large post octavo volumes—to one-fourth of their natural size. Leaves, moreover, lose very little by the process of reduction, because, even in the case of the smaller ones, the reduced figures are large enough to enable the details of the characteristic venation to be clearly seen. But with Ferns the case is different, and the venation of the smaller parts could not be shown unless these were reproduced life-size.

As no adequate representation of natural-sized specimens could be given without space enough to include an entire frond in the case of the majority of the species, the size selected for this work is sixteen by twelve inches. Even within these limits it is, of course, impossible to give the whole frond in the case of such large kinds as the Royal Fern and the Bracken: and, in general, moderately-sized specimens have been selected for purposes of illustration; but where a portion is given of a frond—in two cases only is this volume—that portion is still life-size.

The object of "THE FERN PORTFOLIO" it is repeated, is to give absolutely life-like pictures of Ferns—pictures so true to nature, in every detail, that identification of the specimens figured with others of the same kind will be certain and immediate. Every frond here represented has been carefully collected by the Author, and the delicate and tender handling of the specimens, and the labour incurred in the mere work of laying them down in perfect form, has involved an amount of time in the process scarcely possible to understand except by those who have undertaken a similar task. Then, the work of drawing the detailed outlines of the frond, of putting in the elaborate venation, and of applying the colour with the minute exactness rendered necessary to ensure strict faithfulness of execution, has consumed many months of hard and patient toil.

Whether or not his object has been successfully attained the Author must leave it to the public to determine. He thinks, at least, that he is justified in saying that, be this judgment what it may, no *attempt* has ever been made to give to the public such minutely exact pictures of the fronds of Ferns.

In every case, for the same end—facility of identification—the letterpress descriptions of the Ferns figured has been put exactly facing the figures. It is most important, although it is too seldom done in botanical works, that the illustrations should face the text which they illustrate. By this means tedious reference from one part of the work to another is avoided.

Though specific directions for culture have not been given, the habitats of Ferns have been carefully described, and these will naturally suggest their treatment under cultivation. The more nearly the natural conditions under which Ferns grow can be approached, the more certain will be the success of the cultivator. It need only be added here that Ferns, with few exceptions, like, more or less, moist, but well-drained, sheltered and shady positions, and soil that, light and porous, is rendered rich by the presence in it, in large proportion, of vegetable mould, or the *humus* produced by the decay of leaves.

One important pursuit it is hoped this work will encourage, namely, the study—a most interesting and fascinating one—of the natural conditions under which Ferns grow.

Notwithstanding that every species of British Fern will be found figured and described in this volume, the Ferns included are, it will be seen, quite of a cosmopolitan character, for they are to be met with on the continent of Europe, in the United States, and in other parts of America, in Africa, in Asia, and in the islands of the seas. The list of countries included under the heading of "Distribution" is merely given to show, in a general way, how the Ferns represented are spread over the surface of the world. Whilst, therefore, the work will have, it is hoped, especial interest for readers at home, the Author trusts it will also be welcomed in all English-speaking countries where the beautiful plants it figures are to be found.

FRANCIS GEORGE HEATH.

CONTENTS.

The Fern Plates and accompanying descriptions are not paged, but they appear in the following order :—

First Plate. THE ROYAL FERN—*Osmunda regalis.*
Second   „   THE BROAD BUCKLER FERN—*Lastrea dilatata.*
Third   „   THE BLACK MAIDENHAIR SPLEENWORT—*Asplenium adiantum-nigrum.*
Fourth   „   THE COMMON POLYPODY—*Polypodium vulgare.*
Fifth   „   THE SOFT PRICKLY SHIELD FERN—*Polystichum angulare.*
Sixth   „   THE HART'STONGUE—*Scolopendrium vulgare.*
               THE HAY-SCENTED BUCKLER FERN—*Lastrea recurva.*
               THE RIGID BUCKLER FERN—*Lastrea rigida.*
               THE HARD FERN—*Blechnum spicant.*
Seventh   „   THE MOUNTAIN BUCKLER FERN—*Lastrea montana.*
               THE PRICKLY-TOOTHED BUCKLER FERN—*Lastrea spinulosa.*
Eighth   „   THE LADY FERN—*Athyrium filix-fœmina.*
               THE TRUE MAIDENHAIR—*Adiantum capillus-veneris.*
               THE HOLLY FERN—*Polystichum lonchitis.*
Ninth   „   THE EUROPEAN BRISTLE FERN—*Trichomanes radicans.*
               THE LIMESTONE POLYPODY—*Polypodium calcareum.*
               THE THREE-BRANCHED POLYPODY—*Polypodium dryopteris.*
               THE MOUNTAIN POLYPODY—*Polypodium phegopteris.*
Tenth   „   THE MARSH BUCKLER FERN—*Lastrea thelypteris.*
               THE BRITTLE BLADDER FERN—*Cystopteris fragilis.*
               THE MOUNTAIN BLADDER FERN—*Cystopteris montana.*
               THE SEA SPLEENWORT—*Asplenium marinum.*
Eleventh „   THE BRACKEN—*Pteris aquilina.*
               THE MOONWORT—*Botrychium lunaria.*
               THE ADDER'STONGUE—*Ophioglossum vulgatum.*
               THE LITTLE ADDER'STONGUE—*Ophioglossum lusitanicum.*
Twelfth   „   THE HARD PRICKLY SHIELD FERN—*Polystichum aculeatum.*
               THE ALPINE BLADDER FERN—*Cystopteris regia.*
               THE ANNUAL MAIDENHAIR—*Gymnogramma leptophylla.*
               THE PARSLEY FERN—*Allosurus crispus.*
Thirteenth „   THE ALPINE POLYPODY—*Polypodium alpestre.*
               THE LANCEOLATE SPLEENWORT—*Asplenium lanceolatum.*
               THE SCALY SPLEENWORT—*Asplenium ceterach.*
               THE ROCK SPLEENWORT—*Asplenium fontanum.*
               THE RUE-LEAVED SPLEENWORT—*Asplenium ruta-muraria.*
Fourteenth „   THE CRESTED BUCKLER FERN—*Lastrea cristata.*
               THE COMMON MAIDENHAIR SPLEENWORT—*Asplenium trichomanes.*
               THE GREEN SPLEENWORT—*Asplenium viride.*
               THE ALTERNATE SPLEENWORT—*Asplenium germanicum.*
               THE FORKED SPLEENWORT—*Asplenium septentrionale.*
Fifteenth „   THE MALE FERN—*Lastrea filix-mas.*
               THE OBLONG WOODSIA—*Woodsia ilvensis.*
               THE ALPINE WOODSIA—*Woodsia alpina.*
               THE TUNBRIDGE FILMY FERN—*Hymenophyllum tunbridgense.*
               THE ONE-SIDED FILMY FERN—*Hymenophyllum unilaterale.*

ROYAL FERN—*Osmunda regalis*.

THE ROYAL FERN—*Osmunda regalis*—grows from two to twelve feet high, according to its more or less favourable position. Its roots are fibrous and wiry, and its fronds—of two kinds, barren and fertile—start from a tufted rootstock or trunk, sometimes two feet high. The fronds are deciduous, light green, broadly lance-shaped, bi-pinnate or twice divided, the *pinnæ* or first divisions lance-shaped, and the pinnules—the second and ultimate divisions—oblong and blunt-pointed, broad, and an inch, or more in length. The barren fronds are entirely leafy. The fertile ones, as shown in the present specimen, have their pinnules—mostly in the upper part of the frond only—contracted, and upon them the nearly globular spore cases, brown when ripe, are crowded so thickly as to give the appearance of flowers.

HABITATS.— Banks of lakes and streams, in peaty, boggy soil, and in other low-lying or marshy places.

DISTRIBUTION.—The Azores, Algeria, Belgium, Brazil, British Islands, Canada, China, Croatia, Denmark, France, Germany, Gothland, Holland, Hungary, India, Italy, Japan, Madagascar, Mexico, Natal, Newfoundland, Portugal, Russia, Spain, Sweden, Switzerland, Transylvania, Turkey, and United States.

It is obviously impossible to give within a moderate compass, a full (i.e. a complete) figure of one frond of *Osmunda regalis*: and the upper part only of a fertile frond is here given; but it is natural size and an absolute *facsimile* of the subject from which it is taken. The lower *pinnæ* are longer than the upper ones.

ROYAL FERN.

ROYAL FERN---*OSMUNDA REGALIS.*

HEATH'S FERN PORTFOLIO.

BROAD BUCKLER FERN.—*Lastrea dilatata.*

GROWING in freedom, THE BROAD BUCKLER FERN—*Lastrea dilatata*—is amongst the most stately of the Flowerless Plants, often attaining a height of five or six feet, and spreading and arching its broad, handsome fronds in a manner that is exceedingly beautiful. Oftentimes, however, mature specimens may be found no more than a foot long, and the size varies from that to the maximum length, according to less or more favourable conditions. Its rootstock is large and tufted, and the rootlets are fibrous and abundant. The scales at the base of the frond are mostly few in number, and are dark coloured. The elaborate sub-divisions of the leafy part of the frond, together with the regular and symmetrical arrangement of the whole, give it its especial grace and elegance. The frond, in general form, is broadly lance-shaped, though nearly triangular—from being broadest at the base of the leafy part, whence it tapers upwards. The *pinnae*, or first divisions, mostly set in opposite pairs on the *rachis*, or principal mid stem, are triangular below and lance-shaped higher up on the frond. They, in turn, are again divided into oblong, somewhat blunt-pointed, opposite or alternate, and very elegantly-formed pinnules, or second divisions, which are in turn divided into lobes, the edges of whose indentations are spined. It will be noticed that the lower rows of pinnules on the lower part of the frond are longer than the upper ones, and more divided, making the frond tri-pinnate, or three times divided. The spore cases, collected into *sori*, or little heaps, are scattered over the entire under surface of the frond, each *sorus*, or little heap, being so small as not to be very conspicuous. A deep, rich green is the prevailing colour of this fern, and the pinnules, being concave on their under sides, the fronds have a crisped or curled appearance.

HABITATS.—Great shade and moisture, with a rich soil of leaf mould, provide the most favourable conditions of growth for *Lastrea dilatata*. Hence deep woods, the sloping sides of sheltered lanes, and the shaded nooks of stream sides, are its favourite *habitats*.

DISTRIBUTION.—The Broad Buckler Fern is found in the following parts of the world, namely :—In the Azores, Bourbon, British Islands, Canada, Croatia, France, Germany, Italy, Kamtschatka, Lapland, Mingrelia, Norway, Portugal, Rocky Mountains, Sitka, Spain, Switzerland, Transylvania, and United States. Where the general conditions of growth are favourable to it, it is mostly found growing in great abundance and luxuriance, and no position for displaying its graceful habits suits it so well as the side of a steep slope.

BROAD BUCKLER FERN.

BROAD BUCKLER FERN—*LASTREA DILATATA.*

BLACK MAIDENHAIR SPLEENWORT.

Asplenium adiantum-nigrum.

NO FERN adds a greater degree of beauty and gracefulness to its surroundings than THE BLACK MAIDENHAIR SPLEENWORT — *Asplenium adiantum-nigrum*—and few plants equal it in its rich and glossy loveliness. Suiting its form, its size, and the extent of its attractions to the character of its surroundings, it dwindles, on dry, sunny, exposed situations on rocks or walls, to a tiny thing, an inch, it may be, in length. Where moist seams of earth and shady corners offer it a home it is of larger growth, whilst in such congenial spots under the shelter of overhanging bushes it will become developed till its fronds reach a length, stem and leafy part together, of two feet. Yet its common length is no more than six or nine inches. From a dark, tufted, scaly rootstock the fronds grow somewhat sparingly with a large proportionate length of *stipes*,—or leaf stalk, as it may be called. The stipes is purplish near the base, and greener higher up towards the leafy part, though sometimes remaining purple, becoming green as it merges into the *rachis*, or main stem of the leafy part. The leafy part is triangular in form, and each of the alternately placed *pinnæ*, or second divisions of the frond, is more or less triangular. The pinnules, or second divisions of the leafy parts, are various in form but are mostly somewhat pyramidal on a small scale, and they, in turn, are divided into deeply cut fringed or indented lobes—the ultimate divisions of the frond. The *sori*, or collections of spore-cases on the undersides of the fronds, are arranged in oblique lines, and though distinct when young and green, afterwards become confluent, *i.e.*, run into each other, as they ripen into the dark, rich-brown masses, which, sometimes nearly covering the undersides of the fronds, finely contrast with the warm hue of the stem, and the sheen of the verdant and glossy leafy parts.

HABITATS.—Walls, rocks, ruins, bridge arches, garden enclosures and house walls, and stony banks of all kinds, becoming luxuriant and especially large and beautiful where leaf mould has gathered into the crevices it loves.

DISTRIBUTION.—Abyssinia, Afghanistan, Algiers, Arabia, Armenia, Austria, Azores, Balearic Islands, Belgium, British Islands, Cape of Good Hope, Croatia, Cape de Verd Islands, Corsica, Cyprus, Dalmatia, Denmark, France, Germany, Greece, Hungary, Italy, Java, Madeira, Natal, Porto Rico, Portugal, Russia, Sandwich Isles, Scandinavia, Sicily, Sinai, Spain, Switzerland, Syria, Teneriffe, Transylvania, Turkey, and Virginia.

BLACK MAIDENHAIR SPLEENWORT.

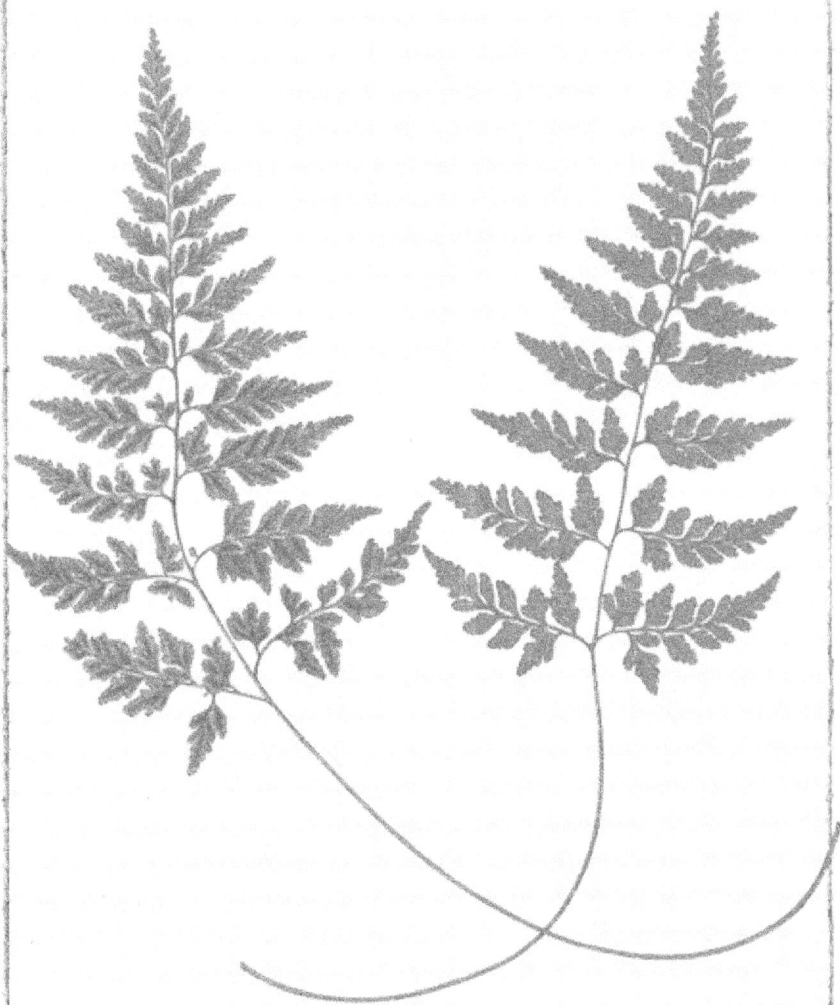

BLACK MAIDENHAIR SPLEENWORT—*ASPLENIUM ADIANTUM NIGRUM.*

HEATH'S FERN PORTFOLIO.

COMMON POLYPODY—*Polypodium vulgare.*

HOW much beauty there is in very common things is shown at no time perhaps more conspicuously than by THE COMMON POLYPODY—*Polypodium vulgare*—when, in the late summer and in early autumn, its mellow fruit crowds in serried lines and in rich profusion upon the light green undersides of its fronds, as they wave in the breeze from the nooks and corners of their favourite habitats. Very different is this simple, but always beautiful, fern in the different places in which it chooses to grow. A spore may drop upon a tiny seam of earth in rock or wall just moist enough to make it grow, but with conditions not sufficiently favourable to encourage development. Then it will remain a minute thing of little more than an inch in length. But on a deeper, richer seam of earth it shows proportionate growth, it may be of six or eight inches; and in the moist fork of a tree in forest or bank it will reach a length of frond sometimes of two feet and a half. From various parts of the upper sides of its scaly, creeping, fleshy *rhizome*, or half subterranean root, it throws up an abundance of delightful fronds, evergreen in sheltered places. These are narrowly or broadly lance-shaped and *pinnatifid*, that is 'cleft like a feather,' or divided into *pinnæ*—or first divisions —nearly down to the mid-stems—the clefts being wide enough to give a very distinctly divided appearance to the leafy part. The pinnæ are an inch and sometimes more in length, and blunt-pointed at their apices. The stipes or stalk is smooth, light-green and herbaceous. The spores are contained in *sori*, or heaps of spore cases, which are round in form, and are gathered in thick, double rows upon the upper undersides of the pinnæ, green whilst young, becoming yellow or brown when ripened.

HABITATS—Rocks, tree stumps, banks, walls, tree forks, hedges, and in innumerable positions where leaf-mould has thickly accumulated.

DISTRIBUTION—Algiers, British Islands, California, Canary Islands, Cape, Erzeroum, France, Germany, Guatemala, Italy, Kamtschatka, Madeira, Mexico, Sardinia, Scandinavia, Sicily, Spain, Switzerland, and United States.

COMMON POLYPODY.

COMMON POLYPODY.—*POLYPODIUM VULGARE.*

HEATH'S FERN PORTFOLIO.

SOFT PRICKLY SHIELD FERN.—*Polystichum angulare.*

EVERGREEN in sheltered positions, THE SOFT PRICKLY SHIELD FERN— *Polystichum angulare*—not unfrequently attains a length of four feet, though from one to two feet is a common size. Few ferns include so much beauty of form and colouring within their own fronds as this species—the most conspicuous feature in which is the fine contrast afforded by the vivid green of the leafy parts, and the rich rust-colouring of the abundant scales which not only thickly clothe the *stipes*—as the frond stalk is called—but the *rachis*—or continuation, through the leafy part, of this stalk. From the rachis, or mid-stem of the leafy part, the scales often thickly extend along the mid-stems of the *pinnæ*, or first divisions of the frond, both on their under and upper sides, though they are more thickly scattered on the under sides. The surfaces of the *lobes*, or ultimate divisions of the leafy part of the frond, often have smaller scales scattered over them. The stipes is usually much shorter than the leafy part and often an inch or two only in length. Upon the crown of the root stock, which is large and tufted, the fronds usually grow in a circle shuttle-cock shape, and, as they are thrown upwards and outwards, assume a lax, and graceful habit. The fronds are lance-shaped and *bi-pinnate*, or twice divided : the *pinnæ*, or first divisions, in opposite pairs or alternate, generally the latter, on the rachis, are also narrowly lance-shaped, and their lobes or divisions—the second divisions of the frond, alternate upon the secondary *rachides* or mid-stems of the pinnæ— are angular, indented and spined. The spores are produced in two short rows, one on each side of the mid-vein of each pinnule ; they are chiefly confined to the upper half of the under side of the frond, and frequently densely cover the surface, giving it a distinct and rich brown hue.

HABITATS—Shady banks of all kinds, the hedges or other borderings of roadsides, the sloping grounds of woods, and almost any moist, shaded and sheltered positions, where overhanging or adjacent vegetation has induced a plentiful supply of the rich mould provided by decaying leaves—for the Soft Prickly Shield Fern loves especially a deep rich soil of vegetable earth into which its strong, wiry rootlets can plunge.

DISTRIBUTION.—*Polystichum angulare* is frequently very abundant in the localities it prefers. It is found in Abyssinia, the Azores, on the Black Sea Coasts, in the British Islands, Canary Islands, Caraccas, France, Georgia, Granada, Greece, Guatemala, India, Italy, Java, Madeira, Mexico, Natal, New Granada, Norway, Singapore, Sitka, Spain, Sweden, and the United States.

SOFT PRICKLY SHIELD FERN.

SOFT PRICKLY SHIELD FERN—*POLYSTICHUM ANGULARE.*

HEATH'S FERN PORTFOLIO.

HARTSTONGUE—*Scolopendrium vulgare.* Fig. 1.
HAY-SCENTED BUCKLER FERN—*Lastrea recurva.* Fig. 2.
RIGID BUCKLER FERN—*Lastrea rigida.* Fig. 3.
HARD FERN—*Blechnum spicant.* Figs. 4 and 5.

ITS name is sufficiently descriptive of the tongue-shaped frond of THE HARTSTONGUE—*Scolopendrium vulgare.* From a stout, tufted rootstock, the evergreen fronds grow abundantly, ranging from an inch or two to three feet in length. A few scales are scattered on the lower part of the *stipes.* The base of the leafy part is auricled on each side of the mid-rib, which, from this point to the pointed frond apex, is very stout and prominent. The *sori,* on the underside, run in parallel lines obliquely from the mid-vein, each conspicuous line consisting of two *sori* placed side by side so closely as to look like one elongated *sorus.* HABITATS.—Rocky places, walls, hedge-banks, streamsides, and woods. DISTRIBUTION.—Algeria, Azores, British Islands, Caucasian Mountains, Erzeroum, European countries generally, Gothland, Madeira, Mexico, Persia, Turcomania, United States, and Ural Mountains.

THE HAY-SCENTED BUCKLER FERN—*Lastrea recurva*—reveals by its beautiful scent of hay the origin of its name. Its fronds, which reach a length of from one foot to two, bear a strong resemblance in form, though not in size, to those of *Lastrea dilatata,* already described. They are triangular, with—first—triangular, and then (higher up) lance-shaped *pinnæ,* divided into oblong, blunted pinnules, which, in the lower part of the frond, are again divided into oblong, serrated lobes, and higher up are merely serrated, the lower pinnules on the lower *pinnæ* being longer than the upper ones. The lobes throughout are recurved, or concave on their upper sides, and the *sori* occur in lines along the mid-veins of the lobe or pinnule undersides. HABITATS.—Moist sheltered woods, and the dampest, richest recesses of hedgebanks. DISTRIBUTION.—Azores, British Islands, Cape de Verd Islands, and Madeira.

A CERTAIN rigidity in its habit of growth makes appropriate the name given to THE RIGID BUCKLER FERN—*Lastrea rigida.* Its fronds, varying from one to two feet in length, are triangular, and are divided into narrowly triangular *pinnæ,* which are in pairs, or alternate, and are divided into oblong, bluntly serrated pinnules, those in the lower parts of the lower *pinnæ* being longer than the upper ones. The *sori* are produced in lines on each side of the mid-veins of the pinnules or *pinnæ.* HABITATS.—Rocky positions in limestone districts. DISTRIBUTION.—Asia Minor, Calabria, California, Croatia, Dalmatia, England, France, Germany, Hungary, Ireland, the Morea, Sardinia, Siberia, Sicily, Switzerland, and United States.

TWO distinct kinds of frond—barren, growing from six inches to two feet, and fertile, from one to three feet—are produced by THE HARD FERN—*Blechnum spicant*—an evergreen, leathery, and fitly-named fern. Narrow and lance-shaped, the *pinnæ* in both fronds are oblong, blunt pointed, widest at the base, and usually connected there by a leafy wing running along the *rachis.* In both fronds the *pinnæ* narrow towards the frond base and the frond apex, but those of the fertile fronds are much more attenuated, usually longer, and have their points curved upwards. The spore cases are so abundantly produced in lines on each side of the mid-veins of the *pinnæ,* that when their growth bursts the *indusium* which protects them, they become confluent, and densely cover the whole underside of the fertile frond, giving it a rich brown appearance. HABITATS.—Moist sloping woodsides, moist lane-banks, and stream banks. DISTRIBUTION.—Africa, America, (North-west) Australia, Azores, British Islands, Canaries, Chili, Europe generally, Japan, Madeira, and Teneriffe.

HARTSTONGUE.

HAY-SCENTED BUCKLER FERN.

RIGID BUCKLER FERN.

HARD FERN.

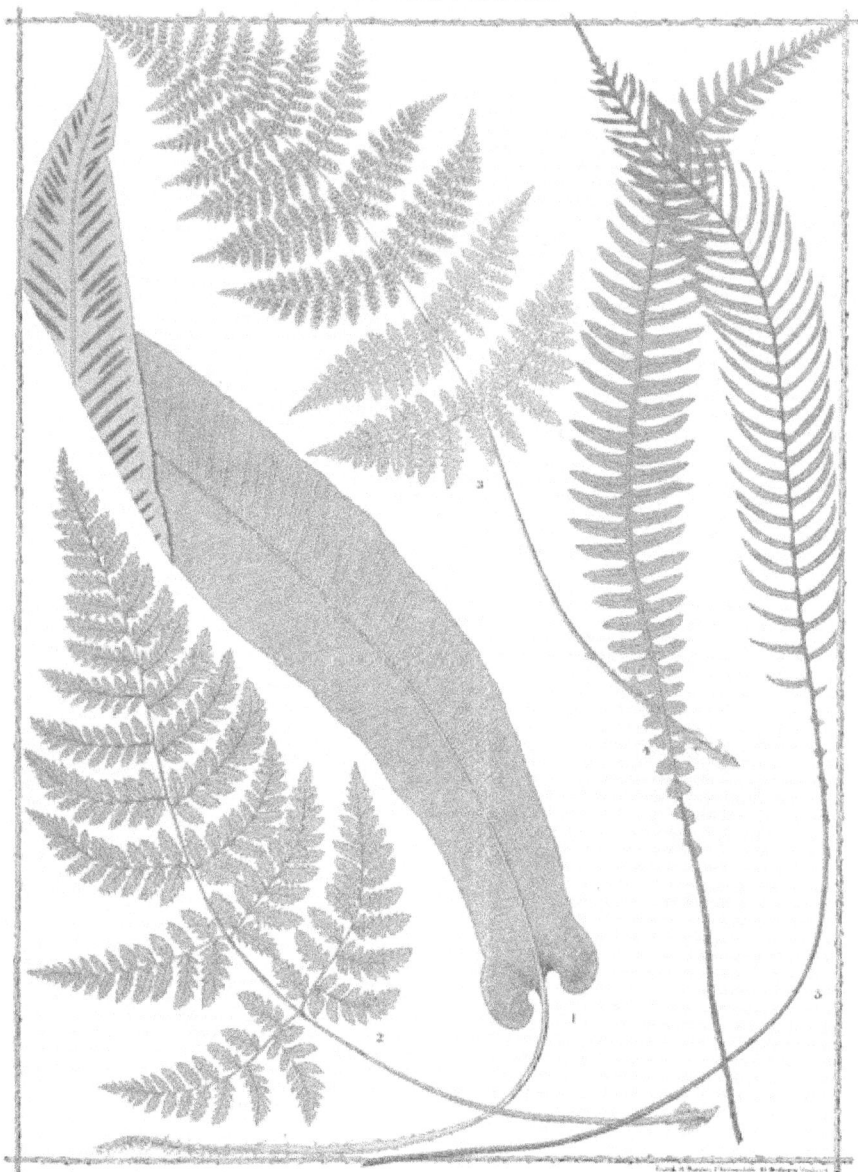

1.—HARTSTONGUE—*SCOLOPENDRIUM VULGARE* (Upper and Under Iron).   2.—HAY-SCENTED BUCKLER FERN—*LASTREA RECURVA* (Upper Iron).

3.—RIGID BUCKLER FERN—*LASTREA RIGIDA* (Under Iron).   4.—HARD FERN—*BLECHNUM SPICANT* (Barren Frond, Upper Iron).   5.—HARD FERN—

BLECHNUM SPICANT (Fertile Frond, Under Iron).

HEATH'S FERN PORTFOLIO.

MOUNTAIN BUCKLER FERN—*Lastrea montana.* Fig. 1.
PRICKLY-TOOTHED BUCKLER FERN—*Lastrea spinulosa.* Fig. 2.

REGIONS more or less mountainous produce THE MOUNTAIN BUCKLER FERN —*Lastrea montana.* From a stout rootstock, golden-green fronds—a foot to four-and-a-half feet long—are abundantly produced. These are deciduous and lance-shaped, but they taper at both ends, and especially towards the base, where the *pinnæ*, nearly in opposite pairs dwindle rapidly in size, until they become, sometimes, mere leafy points. The *stipes* is short, and covered with light-coloured scales. The shorter, basal, *pinnæ* are somewhat triangular ; the longer ones taper to a point from their bases, and are deeply cleft (nearly to the mid-stem) into short, obtuse, smooth-edged pinnules. The round clusters of spore cases occur in lines on each side of the mid-veins of the pinnules, and are more abundant on the upper parts of the undersides of the fronds. HABITATS.—Open mountain sides, damp mountainous woods, and banks of high moorland streams. DISTRIBUTION.—Belgium, British Islands, Croatia, Denmark, France, Germany, Greece, Holland, Hungary, Italy, Norway, Russia, Spain, Switzerland, and Transylvania.

THE PRICKLY-TOOTHED BUCKLER FERN—*Lastrea spinulosa*—has a tufted rootstock, which spreads into numerous crowns. The fronds—a foot to three feet in length—are numerous, nearly triangular, the stipes very long, and scaly, at the base, the *pinnæ* also nearly triangular, and placed in somewhat irregular alternation on the *rachis*. The pinnules are sharply indented and spined, and somewhat egg-shaped, the lower ones of each *pinna*, near the main rachis, being longer than the upper ones, and more deeply indented, the longest being again divided into sharply spined lobes. The spines are turned towards the apices of the pinnules. The spore cases, in their round clusters, are arranged in lines along the mid-veins either of the *pinnæ*, pinnules, or lobes, according to their size and development (an arrangement which is more or less noticeable in all ferns), and they cover, usually, the entire underside of the frond. HABITATS.—Damp, marshy, or boggy positions in woods, where the ground is mossy from abundant and continuous moisture. DISTRIBUTION.—Africa (South), America (North), Asia (North-east), British Islands, and Europe generally, with the exception of the countries of Greece and Turkey.

MOUNTAIN BUCKLER FERN.

PRICKLY-TOOTHED BUCKLER FERN.

1.—MOUNTAIN BUCKLER FERN—*LASTREA MONTANA* (Grass form)   2.—PRICKLY-TOOTHED BUCKLER FERN—*LASTREA SPINULOSA* (Grass form)

HEATH'S FERN PORTFOLIO.

LADY FERN—*Athyrium filix-fœmina.* Fig. 1.

TRUE MAIDENHAIR—*Adiantum capillus-veneris.* Fig. 2.

HOLLY FERN—*Polystichum lonchitis.* Figs. 3. and 4.

PERHAPS the most beautiful of the larger and commoner herbaceous ferns—THE LADY FERN—*Athyrium filix-fœmina*—is found from one to five feet in length of frond. The fronds are abundant (growing from a stout tufted rootstock), lance-shaped, bright green, brittle, and very graceful. They are bi-pinnate, or twice divided, the *stipes*, or stem, being of varying lengths. The *pinnæ*, on the leafy part of the frond, are narrowly lance-shaped, and are placed in opposite pairs, or in irregular alternation, on the *rachis*, and are again divided into pairs of oblong, somewhat blunted, and deeply and sharply indented pinnules. The undersides of the pinnules, which are mostly concave, have the *seri* arranged in lines, one line on each side of the mid-vein of each pinnule. HABITATS.—Damp, shady parts of woods, stream banks, the sides of deep sheltered lanes, and almost any tolerably open but sheltered position where shade and moisture exist and a leaf-mould soil abounds. DISTRIBUTION.—Algiers, America (North, and the northern part of South America), Asia (Russian), Australia, Belgium, British Islands, Canary Islands, Caucasus Mountains, Crete, Croatia, Cuba, France, Germany, Greece, Holland, Hungary, India, Italy, Lapland, Madeira, Mediterranean Islands, Portugal, Russia, Scandinavia, Siberia, Spain, Switzerland, Teneriffe, Transylvania, and the Ural Mountains.

THE TRUE MAIDENHAIR.—*Adiantum capillus-veneris*—is evergreen, and grows from six inches to two feet in height. *Stipes* and leafy part vary in proportionate lengths. The former is purplish and shining, and the *rachis* and its subdivisions are of the same colour, but delicate and hair-like. The leafy part is mostly triangular, the *pinnæ* alternately placed along the rachis, and again divided into alternately-placed pinnules, which, on short, hair-like stems, bear the alternately-placed fan-shaped, and more or less deeply-notched, lobes. The under edge of the lobe-divisions in the fertile fronds are turned down, forming a covering for the *seri*, which thus almost fringe the lobe edges. HABITATS.—Limestone rocks on sea coasts, in positions where shelter, in rocky crevices or under bushes, provides shade, and trickling or oozing water gives sufficient moisture. DISTRIBUTION.—Abyssinia, Alabama, Algiers, Algoa Bay, America (South), Arkansas, Azores, Belgium, British Islands, Caledonia, California, Cape de Verd Islands, Caraccas, Caucasus, Chili, China, Dalmatia, Dominica, Egypt, Florida, France, Greece, Guatemala, India, Jamaica, Java, Madagascar, Madeira, Mascaren Islands, Mexico, New Hebrides, Persia, Portugal, St. Vincent, Sandwich Islands, Siberia, Spain, Switzerland, Syria, Teneriffe, Texas, Trinidad, and Turkey.

ITS spinœd and glossy appearance, and stiff though beautiful regularity of form, give to the name of THE HOLLY FERN—*Polystichum lonchitis*—its especial appropriateness. The root-stock, scaly and tufted, produces fronds which grow from six inches to two feet in length. Their form is narrowly lance-shaped. The *stipes* is very short and scaly, and the *pinnæ* are placed alternately along on each side of the *rachis*. They are distinctly wing-shaped, sharply serrated, and scaly underneath, the lobe-like projection, upwards, of each *pinna* overlapping frequently the base of the preceding *pinna*. The round heaps of spore cases are arranged in lines, on each side of the mid-veins of the *pinnæ*, and are confined to the upper part of the underside of the frond. HABITATS.—Rocky crevices of mountainous regions. DISTRIBUTION.—Altai Mountains, America (North), Asia Minor, Britain, Denmark, France, Germany, Greece, Hungary, Iceland, Ireland, Italy, Kamtschatka, Kashmir, Lapland Russia, Spain, Sweden and Switzerland.

LADY FERN.
TRUE MAIDENHAIR.
HOLLY FERN.

1.—LADY FERN—*ATHYRIUM FILIX-FEMINA* (Grass Size). 2.—TRUE MAIDENHAIR—*ADIANTUM CAPILLUS-VENERIS* (Grass Size). 3.—HOLLY FERN—

POLYSTICHUM LONCHITIS (Grass Size). 4.—HOLLY FERN—*POLYSTICHUM LONCHITIS* (Grass Size).

HEATH'S FERN PORTFOLIO.

EUROPEAN BRISTLE FERN—*Trichomanes radicans*. Fig. 1.
LIMESTONE POLYPODY—*Polypodium calcareum*. Fig. 2.
THREE-BRANCHED POLYPODY—*Polypodium dryopteris*. Fig. 3.
MOUNTAIN POLYPODY—*Polypodium phegopteris*. Fig. 4.

FROM a black scaly *rhizoma*, or creeping root, THE EUROPEAN BRISTLE FERN—*Trichomanes radicans*—throws up evergreen fronds six inches to a foot and a half in length. They are triangular, with narrowly triangular *pinnæ* arranged mostly in pairs, and divided into oblong, alternately-placed pinnules, which are again parted into deeply-cleft lobes. The *pinnæ* and pinnules overlap each other, and the whole aspect of the frond is remarkable by the elaborateness and beauty of its crisped and curled arrangement, and by the semi-pellucid character of its leafy parts—leafy wings bordering, on each side, *stipes*, *rachis*, and the branches and ramifications of the latter. The spores are contained in urn-shaped receptacles on the frond margins. HABITATS.—Dripping rocks in deep shade, in positions where the atmosphere is always charged with moisture. DISTRIBUTION.—Azores, Brazil, Canary Islands, England, Galapagos, India, Ireland, Jamaica, Martinique, Mexico, New Granada, Panama, Sandwich and Society Islands, Spain, Teneriffe, Venezuela, and Wales.

THE LIMESTONE POLYPODY—*Polypodium calcareum*—varies from eight to eighteen inches in length. It has a stout, long, brittle *stipes*, and a triangular leafy part, with *pinnæ* in opposite pairs, the lowest pair larger and more divided than the others, and having opposite or alternated pinnules deeply cleft into blunt, oblong lobes, around the edges of which, in lines, are the *sori*, uncovered, as in the Polypodies in general, by *indusia* or shields. In the next pair of *pinnæ* the division is into indusated pinnules only, and the *pinnæ* upwards gradually dwindle in size and in division. HABITATS.—Moist, rocky crevices in limestone districts. DISTRIBUTION.—Canada, France, Germany, Great Britain, Himalayas, Hungary, Norway, Switzerland, and United States.

DISTINCTLY triangular, with long *stipes*, the fronds of THE THREE-BRANCHED POLYPODY—*Polypodium dryopteris*—spring from a creeping *rhizoma*, and vary from six inches to a foot in length. This fern is deciduous, its lowermost *pinnæ*—a right-angled pair—much larger than the succeeding ones, and divided into opposite pairs of blunt, oblong pinnules, cleft into blunt, oblong lobes. The lower pinnules (near the main *rachis*) of the basal *pinnæ* are longer than the upper ones, and the higher pairs of *pinnæ* are divided into short, blunt lobes, which become smaller and smaller towards the frond apex. The spores are thinly scattered along the mid-veins of the lobes, pinnules, or *pinnæ*. HABITATS.—Mountainous woods and stream margins, in moist, sheltered, and more or less rocky positions. DISTRIBUTION.—Africa, America (North), Asia, British Islands, and European countries, except Greece and Turkey.

TRIANGULAR also and deciduous, THE MOUNTAIN POLYPODY — *Polypodium phegopteris*—differs from other Polypodies in the form of its *pinnæ*. These are long and tapering, longest at the base, and, in the basal pairs, tapering at both ends, the lowermost often drooping. The *pinnæ* are more or less, according to size, deeply cleft into blunted pinnules, and the *sori* are abundantly scattered in lines, one on each side of the mid-vein of each pinnule or *pinna* according to size and development. HABITATS.—Damp woods and streamsides in hilly country, especially near waterfalls. DISTRIBUTION.—Altai Mountains, America (North), Asia (in certain parts), British Islands, Europe generally, and Kamtschatka.

EUROPEAN BRISTLE FERN.

LIMESTONE POLYPODY.

THREE·BRANCHED POLYPODY.

MOUNTAIN POLYPODY.

1.—EUROPEAN BRISTLE FERN—*TRICHOMANES RADICANS* (Upper Scene)   2.—LIMESTONE POLYPODY—*POLYPODIUM CALCAREUM* (Upper Scene)

3.—THREE-BRANCHED POLYPODY—*POLYPODIUM DRYOPTERIS* (Upper Scene)   4.—MOUNTAIN POLYPODY—*POLYPODIUM PHEGOPTERIS* (Upper Scene)

HEATH'S FERN PORTFOLIO.

MARSH BUCKLER FERN—*Lastrea thelypteris*. Fig. 1.
BRITTLE BLADDER FERN—*Cystopteris fragilis*. Fig. 2.
MOUNTAIN BLADDER FERN—*Cystopteris montana*. Fig. 3.
SEA SPLEENWORT—*Asplenium marinum*. Figs. 4 and 5.

THE MARSH BUCKLER FERN—*Lastrea thelypteris*—has two kinds of fronds, barren and fertile; the former, from one to three feet long, being lance-shaped, light green, delicate, herbaceous, with alternately-placed, rather distant, narrowly lance-shaped *pinnæ*, cleft into short, oblong, blunted pinnules, mostly connected by a basal leafy wing. The fertile fronds are similar, but longer, sometimes four feet, and having contracted lobes bearing underneath circular heaps—*sori*—of spore cases along all the lobe edges. HABITATS.—Marshes and other boggy places, growing often in bog water, and preferring the shelter of trees. DISTRIBUTION.—Algiers, America (North and South), North-western Asia, Atlantic Ocean Islands (including British Islands), Cape of Good Hope, New Zealand.

A DELICATE herbaceousness and a tendency to break easily give to THE BRITTLE BLADDER FERN — *Cystopteris fragilis* — its specific name. Its broadly lance-shaped fronds—divided into irregularly alternate, somewhat triangular *pinnæ*, which are again parted into irregularly alternate, irregularly oblong, pinnules (cleft into serrated lobes)—grow thickly from its tufted rootstock to lengths of from six to fourteen inches. The clusters of spore cases—each cluster covered by the bladder-like *indusium*, or cover—are densely scattered over the under-sides of the fronds. HABITATS.—Limestone rocks, in damp and shady crevices, and, less frequently, the walls of buildings. DISTRIBUTION.—Abyssinia, Afghanistan, Altai Mountains, Asia Minor, Azores, Bahamas, California, Canada, Canary Islands, Cape of Good Hope, Chili, Columbia, Cuba, Europe generally (including England, Ireland, Scotland, and Wales, Grenada, Guatemala, Himalayan and Kashmir Mountains, Jamaica, Kamtschatka, Labrador, Madeira, Mexico, Nepal, New Granada, Peru, Quito, Siberia, Simla, Tasmania, Teneriffe, Thibet, United States, and Ural Mountains.

THE MOUNTAIN BLADDER FERN — *Cystopteris montana* — grows from a creeping rootstock, from four to ten inches in length. The *stipes* or stalk is twice as long, usually, as the leafy part which is triangular. The *pinnæ* decrease in size upwards, the lower pinnules of each *pinna* being mostly longer than the upper ones; but the disproportion diminishes upwards, and, towards the apex, disappears. The oblong lobes are deeply cleft below—the indentations diminishing upwards towards the frond tip. The hood-covered *sori* are scattered upon the whole underside of the frond. HABITATS.—Rocky nooks in moist mountainous localities, especially in positions where water trickles along the rocky surfaces. DISTRIBUTION.—America (North), Asia, Denmark, France, Germany, Hungary, Italy, Kamtschatka, Lapland, Norway, Rocky Mountains, Scotland, Spain, Sweden, Switzerland, and Wales (North).

EVERGREEN, like the rest of its genus, THE SEA SPLEENWORT—*Asplenium marinum*—is distinguished by its stout leathery texture. Its length ranges from six inches to three feet. The *stipes* is mostly purple, the *rachis* partly purple and partly green. The leafy part is narrow and strap-shaped, or bluntly lance-shaped, and the *pinnæ*, alternate on the *rachis*, and connected by a narrow leafy wing, are ear-shaped. The *sori*, on the under-side, are arranged in oblique lines. HABITATS.—Sea cliffs and rocks near the sea, in moist shady positions. DISTRIBUTION.—Coasts of Africa (North), America (North), Australia, Azores, Barbary, Bermudas, British Islands, Canary Islands, Corsica, France, Ionian Isles, Italy, Madeira, New Brunswick, New Holland, Portugal, Rio Grande, Spain, and Tangiers.

MARSH BUCKLER FERN.

BRITTLE BLADDER FERN.

MOUNTAIN BLADDER FERN.

SEA SPLEENWORT.

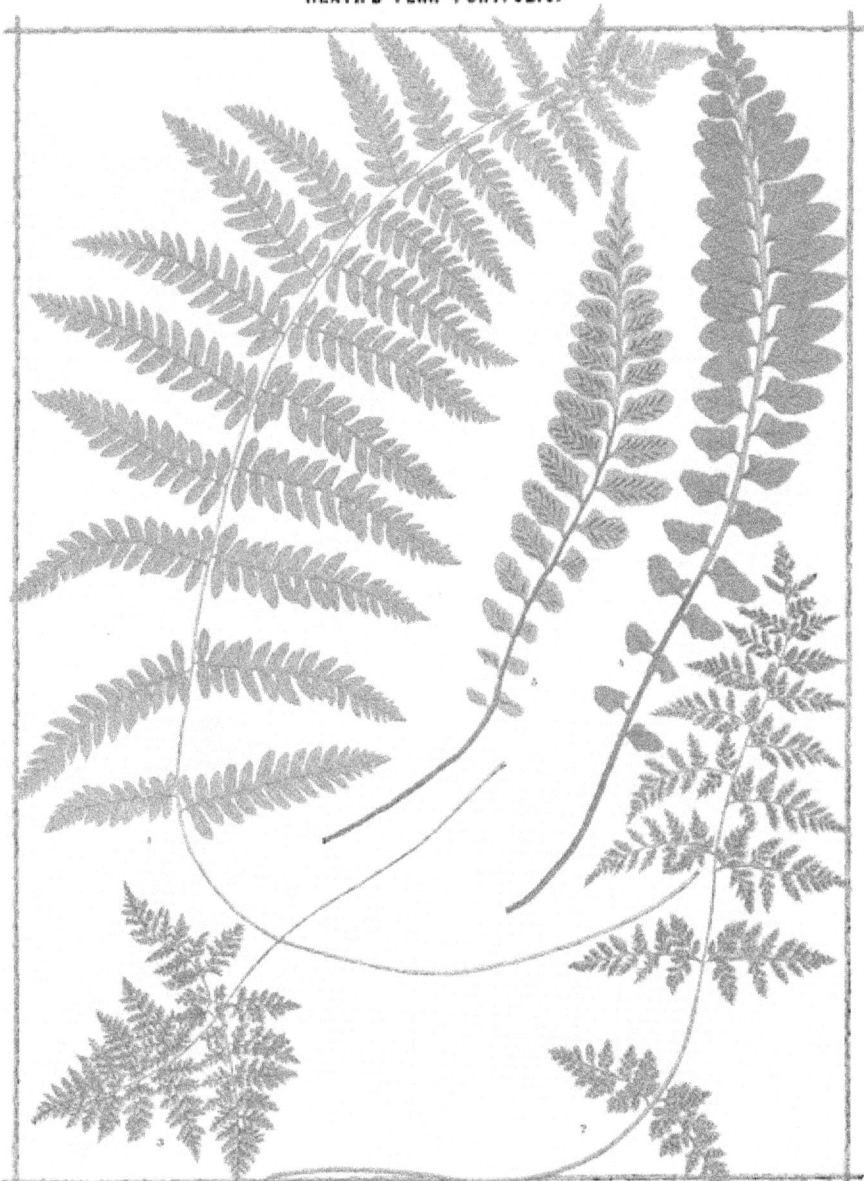

1.—MARSH BUCKLER FERN—*LASTREA THELYPTERIS* (Under Face, Upper Side).   2.—BRITTLE BLADDER FERN—*CYSTOPTERIS FRAGILIS* (Under Side).   3.—MOUNTAIN BLADDER FERN—*CYSTOPTERIS MONTANA* (Under Side).   4.—SEA SPLEENWORT—*ASPLENIUM MARINUM* (Under Side).   5.—SEA SPLEENWORT—*ASPLENIUM MARINUM* (Upper Side).

HEATH'S FERN PORTFOLIO.

BRACKEN—*Pteris aquilina.* Fig. 1.
MOONWORT—*Botrychium lunaria.* Fig. 2.
ADDERSTONGUE—*Ophioglossum vulgatum.* Fig. 3.
LITTLE ADDERSTONGUE—*Ophioglossum lusitanicum.* Fig. 4.

MORE familiar and abundant than any other fern, THE BRACKEN—*Pteris aquilina* —scarcely needs the briefest verbal description. Its fronds are herbaceous, deciduous, dark green, mostly triangular, and grow (from creeping rhizomas) from a foot to twelve in height. They are twice or thrice divided, according to their smaller or larger size. The *pinnæ*, in opposite or alternate pairs on the *rachis*, are triangular near the base and lance-shaped higher up, and are again divided into lance-shaped more or less deeply cleft or smooth-edged pinnules, the divisions of the parts becoming less and less towards the frond apex. The spore cases occur in lines along the edges of the lobes, pinnules, or *pinnæ*, according as they are lower or higher on the frond undersides. *Indusia*, or coverings for the spore cases, are formed by the bent back leafy margins. HABITATS.—Woods, stream banks, open heaths, and hedges. DISTRIBUTION.—Africa, Altai Mountains, America (North and South), Azores, Bourbon, British Islands, California, Canaries, Caucasus, Canada, Ceylon, China, Europe generally, Guatemala, India, Java, Kamtschatka, Madeira, Mauritius, Mexico, the Oriental Archipelago, Penang, Pernambuco, Philippine Islands, Sandwich Islands, Senegambia, Siberia, Sierra Leone, and United States.

A PRETTY and interesting, though an unpretending, little plant, THE MOONWORT— *Botrychium lunaria*—is found from two to ten inches in length. A single frond only, combining a barren and a fertile part, springs from the brittle, succulent, fleshy rootstock. The barren or leafy part consists, above the *stipes*, of pairs of crescents-shaped, entire *pinnæ*. From it diverges the stem of the fertile part, at the upper portion of which are alternate stems of the grape-like clusters of globular spore cases. For the frond figured the Author is indebted to Professor Oliver, of the Kew Herbarium. HABITATS.—Amongst grassy roots, on slightly elevated pastures, heaths, and moors. DISTRIBUTION.—Altai Mountains, British Islands, Canada, Europe generally, Greenland, Himalayas, Kamtschatka, Newfoundland, Rocky Mountains, Siberia, Sitka, Tasmania, Ural Mountains, and Victoria.

SIMPLER in form even than the Moonwort is THE ADDERSTONGUE—*Ophioglossum vulgatum*—the frond of which, usually found growing from four to twelve inches long, consists of a barren or leafy part and of a fertile one—the former being distinctly egg-shaped, and the latter having a stem sheathed by the base of the leafy part, and surmounted by a pointed fruit spike, consisting of two rows of rounded spore cases. HABITATS.—Moist grassy places, on heaths, meadows, and moors. It should be looked for in damper and more loamy positions than the Moonwort, and at a less elevation than the latter. DISTRIBUTION.—Africa, America (North), Australia, British Islands, Caucasian Mountains, East Indies, Europe generally, Kamtschatka, Mexico, New Holland, New Zealand, and Siberia.

A BETTER description could scarcely be given of THE LITTLE ADDERSTONGUE —*Ophioglossum lusitanicum*—than by saying that it is a diminutive likeness of the Adderstongue. Like the latter, it has a frond combining a barren or leafy part and a fruit-bearing spike; but the leafy part is narrower in proportion than is that of *Ophioglossum vulgatum*. It is about an inch altogether in length. For the specimen from which the figure is drawn the Author is indebted to Professor Dyer, of Kew Gardens. HABITATS.—It is found growing amidst grass on commons, heaths, and meadows. DISTRIBUTION.—Algiers, Azores, Canary Islands, Cape de Verde Islands, Dalmatia, France, Greece, Italy, Jersey, Madeira, New Zealand, Portugal, St. Helena, Sicily, Spain, Swan River, Tangiers, and Western Australia.

BRACKEN.

MOONWORT.

ADDERSTONGUE.

LITTLE ADDERSTONGUE.

1.—BRACKEN—*PTERIS AQUILINA* (The Brake or Fern, Corn Fern.)   2.—MOONWORT—*BOTRYCHIUM LUNARIA.*   3.—ADDERSTONGUE—*OPHIOGLOSSUM VULGATUM.*   4.—LITTLE ADDERSTONGUE—*OPHIOGLOSSUM LUSITANICUM.*

HEATH'S FERN PORTFOLIO.

HARD PRICKLY SHIELD FERN—*Polystichum aculeatum*. Fig. 1.
ALPINE BLADDER FERN—*Cystopteris regia*. Fig. 2.
ANNUAL MAIDENHAIR—*Gymnogramma leptophylla*. Figs. 3 and 4.
PARSLEY FERN—*Allosorus crispus*. Figs. 5 and 6.

A RIGID, leathery, but withal graceful aspect, has THE HARD PRICKLY SHIELD FERN—*Polystichum aculeatum*—whose handsome evergreen fronds grow from two to four feet in length. The short *stipes* is scaly; the leafy part lance-shaped, and divided into alternate lance-shaped *pinnæ*, which are again parted into spined, wing-shaped pinnules, the basal pinnule of each *pinna* being more than proportionately larger than the others. The rounded clusters of spore cases are spread in lines on both sides of the mid-veins of the pinnules, but chiefly occur on the upper half of the underside of the frond. The frond figured was obtained from the collection of Professor Dyer, of Kew Gardens. HABITATS.—The higher slopes of woods, the sloping sides of hedge-banks, and the sides of walls skirting streams. DISTRIBUTION.—Africa (South), America (United States), Asia, Austria, Belgium, British Islands, France, Germany, Greece, Holland, Italy, Madeira, Portugal, Russia, Scandinavia, Spain, Switzerland, and Turkey.

BROADLY lance-shaped in form, the beautiful fronds of THE ALPINE BLADDER FERN—*Cystopteris regia*—attain a length of from three to ten inches. The *pinnæ* are irregularly alternated on the *rachis*, are irregularly ovate in form, and are divided into ovate and more or less deeply cleft pinnules. Upon the undersides of these are evenly but somewhat sparsely scattered the hood-covered *sori*. HABITATS.—Rocky fissures and the crevices of old walls. DISTRIBUTION.—Alpine regions of Europe, Asia Minor, Belgium, Britain (England, Scotland, and Wales), Croatia, Dalmatia, France, Greece, Hungary, Italy, Spain, Sweden, and Transylvania.

DISTINGUISHED from all the other ferns described in this volume by its annual habit of growth, THE ANNUAL MAIDENHAIR—*Gymnogramma leptophylla*—dies away as soon as it has completed its purpose by the shedding of its spores. From its tufted rootstock spring pretty, delicate, herbaceous, bright-green fronds, which, as they succeed each other, become, in their three gradations, taller and taller, and vary from three to nine inches in length. The later and more perfect ones, like those figured, are bi-pinnate, or twice divided, and triangular in form, with irregularly-shaped alternate *pinnæ*, parted into pinnules cleft, in turn, into fan-shaped indented lobes. Thickly covering the undersides of these are the non-indusiate lines of spore cases. HABITATS.—Amongst dwarf vegetation on moist banks (facing south) over which ooze some trickling streams of water. DISTRIBUTION.—Abyssinia, Algiers, Azores, Canaries, Cape of Good Hope, France, Germany, Greece, India, Italy, Jersey, Madeira, Mexico, Morocco, New Zealand, Portugal, Sicily, Spain, Switzerland, Tasmania, Vera Cruz, and Victoria.

ITS common name indicates the peculiarity of form of THE PARSLEY FERN—*Allosorus crispus*—which from its tufted rootstock throws up two kinds of frond, barren and fertile. The former, or leafy ones—four to eight inches long—are triangular, and divided into alternately-placed *pinnæ*, parted into alternate wedge-shaped pinnules that are again divided into cleft, wedge-shaped lobes. Precisely the same arrangement is noticeable in the taller fertile fronds; but in these the lobes are much contracted by their edges being bent under to form coverings for the crowded and ultimately confluent spore cases. HABITATS.—Rocky sides of mountainous or hilly country—its abundance in such positions having obtained for it the name of 'rock brakes.' DISTRIBUTION.—America (North), British Islands, Denmark, France, Germany, Hungary, Italy, Lapland, Norway, Sitka, Spain, Sweden, and Switzerland. For fronds for the figures of the three species last named the Author is indebted to Mr. F. W. Stansfield, of Sale.

HARD PRICKLY SHIELD FERN.

ALPINE BLADDER FERN.

ANNUAL MAIDENHAIR.

PARSLEY FERN.

1.—HARD PRICKLY SHIELD FERN—*POLYSTICHUM ACULEATUM* (Cross line)   2.—ALPINE BLADDER FERN—*CYSTOPTERIS ALPINA* (Cross line)
3.—ANNUAL MAIDENHAIR—*GYMNOGRAMMA LEPTOPHYLLA* (Cross line)   4.—ANNUAL MAIDENHAIR—*GYMNOGRAMMA LEPTOPHYLLA* (Cross line)
5.—PARSLEY FERN—*ALLOSORUS CRISPUS* (Under Front)   6.—PARSLEY FERN—*ALLOSORUS CRISPUS* (Upper Front)

HEATH'S FERN PORTFOLIO.

ALPINE POLYPODY—*Polypodium alpestre.* Fig. 1.
LANCEOLATE SPLEENWORT—*Asplenium lanceolatum.* Figs. 2 and 3.
SCALY SPLEENWORT—*Asplenium ceterach.* Figs. 4 and 5.
ROCK SPLEENWORT—*Asplenium fontanum.* Figs. 6 and 7.
RUE-LEAVED SPLEENWORT—*Asplenium ruta-muraria.*
Figs. 8 and 9.

THE fronds of THE ALPINE POLYPODY—*Polypodium alpestre*—are much like those of the Lady Fern, and rise, from an erect rootstock, a foot to three feet and a half. They are broadly lance-shaped and have alternate, narrowly-triangular *pinnæ*, divided into alternate, ovate, indented pinnules. The *sori* on the underside are not covered by *indusia* or shields. For the frond from which the drawing of the accompanying figure was made, the Author is indebted to Mr. F. W. Stansfield, of Sale. HABITATS.—High mountainous regions, chiefly amongst rocks, and in other moist positions. DISTRIBUTION.— The Caucasus, Germany, Lapland, Norway, Russia, Sweden, and Switzerland.

OF the five Spleenworts now to be figured and briefly described THE LANCEOLATE SPLEENWORT—*Asplenium lanceolatum* — takes its name from the form of its fronds. These are evergreen and lance-shaped, having opposite or alternate, bluntly-triangular *pinnæ*, bearing alternate, somewhat four-sided, and more or less deeply cleft, pinnules. The round *sori* assume a regular and semi-triangular shape on the backs of the fronds, and are very abundant. HABITATS.—Sea caves and other moist and rocky positions near the sea. DISTRIBUTION.—Algiers, Azores, Belgium, England, English Channel Islands, France, Germany, Italy, Madeira, Portugal, Sicily, Spain, and Tangiers.

VERY beautiful is the dark green upperside and the brown scaly back of THE SCALY SPLEENWORT—*Asplenium ceterach.* From one to eight inches is its length. The alternate, conical *pinnæ*, present on each side of the *rachis* the appearance of blunt cogs; the *stipes* is very short and scaly, and the space caves, in elongated *sori*, are concealed amongst the dense scaly covering of the undersides of the stout fronds. HABITATS.—Moist crevices of rocks, walls, and bridge arches. DISTRIBUTION.—Algiers, Armenia, Asia Minor, Austria, Azores, Balearic Isles, Belgium, Brazil, British Islands, Canaries, Cape de Verde Islands, Caucasus, Croatia, Dalmatia, Erzeroum, France, Germany, Gothland, Greece, Holland, Hungary, India, Italy, Madeira, Portugal, Russia (South), Siberia, Spain, Switzerland, Thibet, Transylvania, Turkey, and Ural Mountains.

ELEGANTLY lance-shaped in form, the evergreen fronds of THE ROCK SPLEEN-WORT—*Asplenium fontanum*—are found of lengths varying from two or three to twelve inches. The *stipes* is very short and the *pinnæ* are egg-shaped, sharply indented, and placed alternately and very symmetrically along the *rachis.* The *sori* are oblong; they run obliquely from the mid-veins of the *pinnæ*, and they are scattered pretty evenly over the entire underside of the frond. HABITATS.—Shady nooks in rocks, walls, and the sides of sea caves. DISTRIBUTION.—Belgium, British Islands, Cashmere, France, Greece, Hungary, Italy, Siberia, Spain, and Switzerland.

THE RUE-LEAVED SPLEENWORT—*Asplenium ruta-muraria*—bears fronds growing from small tufted rootstocks and ranging from one to six inches in length. They are evergreen, and leathery-textured, and have the *stipes* mostly long, and the leafy part triangular. The *pinnæ* are placed in irregular alternation on each side of the *rachis*, and are divided into curious little club-shaped pinnules, generally in threes. Running in oblique lines upon the frond, the *sori*, as they become ripe, run into each other, and then densely cover the under-surface. HABITATS.—Old walls, rocks, bridge arches, and other stony places. DISTRIBUTION.—Africa, America (North), Asia, Belgium, Bohemia, British Islands, Corsica, Crimea, Croatia, Dalmatia, France, Germany, Greece, Holland, Hungary, Italy, Norway, Portugal, Russia, Scandinavia, Sicily, Spain, Switzerland, Transylvania, and Turkey.

ALPINE POLYPODY.

LANCEOLATE SPLEENWORT.

SCALY SPLEENWORT.

ROCK SPLEENWORT.

RUE-LEAVED SPLEENWORT.

1.—ALPINE POLYPODY—*POLYPODIUM ALPINUM* (Upper Iron). 2.—LANCEOLATE SPLEENWORT—*ASPLENIUM LANCEOLATUM* (Upper Iron). 3.—LANCEOLATE SPLEENWORT—*ASPLENIUM LANCEOLATUM* (Under Iron). 4.—SCALY SPLEENWORT—*ASPLENIUM CETERACH* (Upper Iron). 5.—SCALY SPLEENWORT—*ASPLENIUM CETERACH* (Under Iron). 6.—ROCK SPLEENWORT—*ASPLENIUM FONTANUM* (Upper Iron). 7.—ROCK SPLEENWORT—*ASPLENIUM FONTANUM* (Under Iron). 8.—RUE-LEAVED SPLEENWORT—*ASPLENIUM RUTA MURARIA* (Upper Iron). 9.—RUE-LEAVED SPLEENWORT—*ASPLENIUM RUTA MURARIA* (Under Iron).

HEATH'S FERN PORTFOLIO.

CRESTED BUCKLER FERN—*Lastrea cristata.* Fig. 1.
COMMON MAIDENHAIR SPLEENWORT—*Asplenium trichomanes.*
Figs. 2 and 3.
GREEN SPLEENWORT—*Asplenium viride.* Figs. 4 and 5.
ALTERNATE SPLEENWORT—*Asplenium germanicum.* Figs. 6 and 7.
FORKED SPLEENWORT—*Asplenium septentrionale.* Figs. 8 and 9.

THE fronds of THE CRESTED BUCKLER FERN—*Lastrea cristata*—grow from one to three feet in length. They are irregularly oblong, widest about the middle, the *pinnæ* alternate, triangular, but rounded at the base, and cleft into short, oblong, serrated pinnules, along each under-side of which the *sori* are produced. HABITATS.—Bogs and marshy parts of woods. DISTRIBUTION.—Belgium, Bœotia, Canada, Croatia, England, France, Germany, Holland, Hungary, Russia, Scandinavia, Siberia, Switzerland, Transylvania, and United States. The frond figured was courteously supplied by Professor Dyer, of Kew Gardens.

OF the pretty little series of Spleenworts, now to be described, the first to mention is THE COMMON MAIDENHAIR SPLEENWORT—*Asplenium trichomanes*—which from its tufted rootstock sends up an abundance of evergreen fronds. Stipes and *rachis* are purple throughout, and in pairs, or alternate ; on the latter are produced the small, nearly oval, and usually entire *pinnæ*, which diminish in size both towards the apex and the base of the frond. The oblong *sori* on the undersides densely cover the latter, and as they ripen become confluent. HABITATS.— Moist crevices of rocks, walls, bridge arches, and hedge-banks. DISTRIBUTION.—Afghanistan, Algeria, Altai Mountains, Australia, Azores, Belgium, British Islands, Canada, Cape de Verd Islands, Caucasus, Columbia, Corsica, Crimea, Croatia, Cuba, Dalmatia, France, Germany, Greece, Himalayas, Hungary, Italy, Jamaica, Kaffraria, Kashmir, Madeira, Mexico, New Mexico, Paramatta, Persia, Peru, Portugal, Russia, Sandwich Islands, Scandinavia, Siberia, Sicily, Simla, Spain, Switzerland, Tasmania, Transylvania, Turkey, United States, Ural Mountains, and Venezuela.

THE GREEN SPLEENWORT—*Asplenium viride*—whose fronds are from two to ten inches long, is distinguishable from *Asplenium trichomanes* chiefly by having a green instead of a purple *rachis*. Its *pinnæ*, too, are usually rounder. They are produced in pairs or alternately, and underneath them the *sori* are scattered much less abundantly than on the Common Maidenhair Spleenwort. HABITATS.—Fissures of rocks, in moorland districts where water trickles over the stony surfaces. DISTRIBUTION.—Belgium, Bohemia, British Islands, Columbia, Croatia, Dalmatia, Finland, France, Germany, Greece, India, Italy, Lapland, Norway, Peru, Rocky Mountains, Russia, Siberia, Sitka, Spain, Sweden, and Switzerland.

THE distinct alternation on the *rachis* of its prettily-cleft, club-shaped, leathery, evergreen *pinnæ* is the obvious reason for the name given to THE ALTERNATE SPLEENWORT— *Asplenium germanicum*—whose little fronds grow from two to six inches long. As in all the Spleenworts already described, the oblong *sori* are produced in oblique lines, and often become confluent as they ripen. HABITATS.—Moist, rocky clefts in mountainous districts. DISTRIBUTION.—Belgium, Britain, Carpathians, Croatia, Dalmatia, Finland, France, Germany, Hungary, Italy, Norway, Spain, Sweden, Switzerland, and Tyrol.

EVEN simpler in form and division than the preceding, the fronds of THE FORKED SPLEENWORT—*Asplenium septentrionale*—consist of little grass-like tufts, each frond having a long *stipes* surmounted by a leafy part, forked into three-cleft, club-shaped divisions. Underneath, the crowded *sori* are covered at first by the scale-like indusium attached at each margin, and later on, when ripe, burst their covering and become confluent. HABITATS.—Moist, earthy seams of rocks and walls. DISTRIBUTION.—Belgium, Britain, Denmark, France, Germany, Hungary, India, Italy, Lapland, New Mexico, Portugal, Russia, Scandinavia, Spain, Sweden, and Switzerland. For fronds of the two ferns just mentioned the Author is indebted to Mr. F. W. Stansfield, of Sale.

CRESTED BUCKLER FERN.

COMMON MAIDENHAIR SPLEENWORT.

GREEN SPLEENWORT.

ALTERNATE SPLEENWORT.

FORKED SPLEENWORT.

1.—CRESTED BUCKLER FERN—*LASTREA CRISTATA* (Circa ½ size). 2.—COMMON MAIDENHAIR SPLEENWORT—*ASPLENIUM TRICHOMANES* (Circa ½ size). 3.—COMMON MAIDENHAIR SPLEENWORT—*ASPLENIUM TRICHOMANES* (Circa ½ size). 4.—GREEN SPLEENWORT—*ASPLENIUM VIRIDE* (Circa ½ size). 5.—GREEN SPLEENWORT—*ASPLENIUM VIRIDE* (Circa ½ size). 6.—ALTERNATE SPLEENWORT—*ASPLENIUM GERMANICUM* (Circa ½ size). 7.—ALTERNATE SPLEENWORT—*ASPLENIUM GERMANICUM* (Circa ½ size). 8.—FORKED SPLEENWORT—*ASPLENIUM SEPTENTRIONALE* (Circa ½ size). 9.—FORKED SPLEENWORT—*ASPLENIUM SEPTENTRIONALE* (Circa ½ size).

HEATH'S FERN PORTFOLIO.

MALE FERN—*Lastrea Filix-mas.* Fig. 1
OBLONG WOODSIA—*Woodsia ilvensis.* Figs. 2 and 3.
ALPINE WOODSIA—*Woodsia alpina.* Fig. 4.
TUNBRIDGE FILMY FERN—*Hymenophyllum tunbridgense.* Fig. 5.
ONE-SIDED FILMY FERN—*Hymenophyllum unilaterale.* Fig. 6.

ROBUST looking and vigorous, THE MALE FERN—*Lastrea filix-mas*—well earns its virile name. From its stout rootstock it throws up fronds from one to five feet in length. Root-stock, crown, *stipes* and *rachis*, are densely scaly. The *stipes* is short, the leafy part lance-shaped, and the *pinnæ*, in pairs or alternate, are long, tapering, and more or less deeply cut into short, oblong pinnules. The *sori* occur in short lines parallel with the mid-veins of the latter, on the upper half of the frond underside. HABITATS.—Lanes, streams-banks and woods. DISTRIBUTION. —Africa, America, Asia, Brazil, British Islands, California, Caraccas, Equator, Guatemala, Madeira, Newfoundland, New Granada, and Peru.

ELEGANT in appearance, the fronds of THE OBLONG WOODSIA—*Woodsia ilvensis* —which grow from one to six inches, are shaped in accordance with their name. The *pinnæ*, opposite or alternate, are also oblong and divided into short, oblong lobes. The *sori* appear along the margins of the *pinnæ*. Stipes, rachis, and the whole underside are densely covered with downy hairs. HABITATS.—Moist rocky crevices in mountainous districts. DISTRIBUTION.— America (North, and United States), Britain, Canada, Denmark, France, Germany, Hungary, Iceland, Italy, Kamtschatka, Lapland, Norway, Russia, Siberia, Spain, Sweden, and Switzerland.

ITS smaller size is the chief mark distinguishing THE ALPINE WOODSIA—*Woodsia alpina*—from the Oblong Woodsia. Its length varies from one inch to three. The form of its frond is oblong, and the opposite or alternate *pinnæ* are notched rather than cleft into rounded lobes. The *sori* on the *pinnæ* are arranged on the same plan as in *Woodsia ilvensis*, but the covering of hairs, though similar, is not quite so dense as in that fern. HABITATS.—Crannies of dripping rocks in mountainous regions. DISTRIBUTION.—America (North), Finland, France, Germany, Hungary, Italy, Lapland, Norway, Russia, Scotland, Siberia, Silesia, Spain, Sweden, Switzerland, Transylvania, and Wales.

THE two species of Filmy Ferns now to be described are remarkable for the semi-pellucid character of their ovate leafy parts. Taking first THE TUNBRIDGE FILMY FERN— *Hymenophyllum tunbridgense*—the black hair-like *stipes* of each frond rises from a creeping, hair-like rhizoma, and the dark-green alternate *pinnæ* are irregularly branched and forked on both sides of their mid-veins, much like the branching of coral. The spore cases are contained in urn shaped receptacles borne on the points of veins in the angles of the *pinnæ*. HABITATS.—Dark, dripping rocky holes and rocky surfaces where perpetual moisture is maintained. DISTRIBUTION.—Australian Islands, Azores, Brazil, British Islands, Cape of Good Hope, Chili, France, Germany, India, Italy, Madeira, Mauritius, Norway, New Zealand, Sweden, and Tasmania.

SIMILAR in its general character to the fern just described, the only distinctions worth noticing in THE ONE-SIDED FILMY FERN—*Hymenophyllum unilaterale*—are, that the leafy portion proceeds from one side—and that the upper one—of the mid-vein of each *pinna*, and that the fronds are thus one-sided and narrow. The spore cases are contained in the same kind of urn-shaped receptacles, and the general length of fronds is about the same. HABITATS.—Dark, dripping, rocky holes, often at somewhat higher elevations than those of *Hymenophyllum tunbridgense*. DISTRIBUTION.—Australian Islands, Azores, Brazil, British Islands, Cape of Good Hope, Chili, France, Germany, India, Italy, Madeira, Mauritius, Norway, New Zealand, Sweden, and Tasmania.

MALE FERN.

OBLONG WOODSIA.

ALPINE WOODSIA.

TUNBRIDGE FILMY FERN.

ONE-SIDED FILMY FERN.

1.—MALE FERN—*LASTREA FILIX-MAS* (Cross Size)   3.—OBLONG WOODSIA—*WOODSIA ILVENSIS* (Cross Size)   3.—OBLONG WOODSIA—*WOODSIA ILVENSIS* (Cross Size).   4.—ALPINE WOODSIA—*WOODSIA ALPINA* (Cross Size)   5.—TUNBRIDGE FILMY FERN—*HYMENOPHYLLUM TUNBRIDGENSE.*
6.—ONE-SIDED FILMY FERN—*HYMENOPHYLLUM UNILATERALE.*

www.ingramcontent.com/pod-product-compliance
Lightning Source LLC
Chambersburg PA
CBHW021629270326
41931CB00008B/930